M000022914

SALES MANAGEMENT

BRIAN TRACY

AMACOM AMERICAN MANAGEMENT ASSOCIATION
New York · Atlanta · Brussels · Chicago · Mexico City
San Francisco · Shanghai · Tokyo · Toronto · Washington, D.C.

Bulk discounts available. For details visit:
www.amacombooks.org/go/specialsales
Or contact special sales:
Phone: 800-250-5308 / Email: specialsls@amanet.org
View all the AMACOM titles at: www.amacombooks.org

Library of Congress Cataloging-in-Publication Data

Tracy, Brian.
Sales management / Brian Tracy.
   pages cm
Includes bibliographical references and index.
ISBN 978-0-8144-3629-5 (hardcover : alk. paper) — ISBN 978-0-8144-3630-1 (ebook) 1. Sales management. 2. Leadership. I. Title.
HF5438.4.T73 2015
658.8'1—dc23

                                                              2015009452

About AMA

American Management Association (www.amanet.org) is a world leader in talent development, advancing the skills of individuals to drive business success. Our mission is to support the goals of individuals and organizations through a complete range of products and services, including classroom and virtual seminars, webcasts, webinars, podcasts, conferences, corporate and government solutions, business books, and research. AMA's approach to improving performance combines experiential learning—learning through doing—with opportunities for ongoing professional growth at every step of one's career journey.

Printing number
10 9 8 7 6 5 4 3 2 1

CONTENTS

Introduction

WHEN IBM RAN into financial trouble the early 1990s, the company brought in a new president, Lou Gerstner. He immediately called in his friends from McKinsey & Company, one of the largest and most respected management consultancies in the world. He asked them to use their investigative skills to determine why IBM sales, market share, and profits were falling. They immediately went to work.

In less than six months, the consultants were back. They assembled the senior executives and told them, "We have found your problem."

They asked, "What is it?"

The McKinsey consultants replied, "Low sales."

The executives agreed that this was the problem and then asked, "What is the solution?"

The McKinsey consultants said simply, "High sales."

Again, the senior IBM executives pointed out that these two answers were obvious. But how would these high sales be achieved?

The 75 Percent Rule

The answer became known as the "75 percent rule." In their research, they found that as the result of certain company policies, salespeople and sales managers were spending too much time in the office filling out forms and too little time in the field face-to-face with customers.

They recommended that this situation be reversed immediately. The 75 percent rule simply said that from now on, the salespeople should spend 75 percent of their time in the field with customers talking about IBM products and services. In addition, the sales managers, who had been stuck in their offices most of the day processing the paperwork that the salespeople were generating, were to spend 75 percent of their time in the field with salespeople calling on key customers.

Within a year, IBM's sales reversed completely. Huge losses turned into huge profits. The company turned around and again became a giant of American industry.

The Pivotal Skill

At the end of this study, the McKinsey people explained their most important finding: In a sales-driven organization, the sales manager is the pivotal skill. Nothing will bring about faster and more predictable increases in sales performance and sales results than training sales managers to do their job more effectively.

As a sales manager, you are the most important person in the sales-driven organization. You have more influence on the level of sales and, ultimately, the level of profitability of the company than almost any other person. You are vital to the success of the company.

The sales manager is one of the most valuable and often one of the least appreciated executives in the company. It is the sales manager who sets the standards and quotas for the salespeople and sees that they achieve them. The development of excellent sales managers is an essential requirement for all successful business enterprises.

The Journey Begins

Welcome to *Sales Management*. This book is based on years of experience and study into the attitudes and behaviors of successful sales managers. Throughout the pages ahead, you will learn a series of key ideas, methods, principles, and techniques that you can use, starting immediately, to make your sales force more effective, to produce more sales, to work more harmoniously together, and to advance your own personal career and prestige as rapidly as possible.

Sales management is an inexact science because salespeople are very different from most other employees. A sales manager must be a friend, a counselor, a confidant, a stern taskmaster, and an efficient business-oriented executive, all at the same time.

Salespeople have emotional highs and lows, selling booms and slumps, and a variety of eccentricities that require a person with tremendous patience and superior human relations skills to manage and control them.

The superior sales manager is a person who can mold a variety of different personalities into an effective sales team that can produce predictable and consistent sales results, month after month. Persistent application of the principles taught in this book will allow a sales manager such as yourself to achieve better sales results—starting immediately.

Remember, however, that there are no final answers in dealing with salespeople. There are exceptions to every rule. Because of the complexities of the human personality, an excellent sales manager is always aware that the person facing him across the desk may be an exception, either positive or negative.

With the ideas contained in this book, ambitious sales managers will discover they have more positive, productive people working for them and fewer negative, unproductive people. Let's begin.

ONE

The Role of the Sales Manager

THE NUMBER ONE role of the sales manager is to generate the sales that are essential to the survival of the company. The sales manager achieves these sales results by working with and through other salespeople.

One of your most important jobs is to determine the level of sales you want to achieve daily, weekly, monthly, quarterly, and annually. Establish these goals as your targets and then work back to the present day. Decide what you will have to do to hit those targets in those time spans.

To hit your sales quotas, you will have to plan, project, and organize people, resources, budgets, and promotional materials. You must determine the plans of action that you will follow to get from where you are to where you want to go in terms of sales results. The better planner you are, the more successful you will be, irrespective of what is going on in the marketplace.

Another major responsibility you have is to communicate and motivate. You get your work done through other people. Their results are your results. You need to be able to give your people the information, resources, and incentives they need to get their jobs done.

Your next key function is to measure results. One of the most important business principles is this: "What gets measured gets done." If you can't measure it, you can't manage it. If you don't measure it, it's probably not going to get done at all. That's why you need clear objectives, standards of performance, and assigned responsibilities for every person.

Choose the Right People

Perhaps your most important job is to select, recruit, and hire good salespeople. Fully 95 percent of your success will be determined by the quality of the people you hire in the first place. We will talk about your selection of salespeople in detail in Chapter 3.

You must teach, train, develop, and build your salespeople so that, no matter how long they stay with you, when and if they leave, they will be more competent, capable, and effective human beings than they were when they arrived.

Your final major responsibility is to determine the resources necessary for you to accomplish all of the above. Your job as a sales manager makes you responsible for setting and achieving sales goals. This means that you have to determine the sales plan, the training materials, the budgets, the rewards, the incentives, and the sales campaigns. You also have to organize the work and prepare forecasts in each case.

Sometimes, some of these jobs will be done for you, and sometimes they will be your responsibility alone, but at the end of the day, results are everything. You have to determine the products you are going to focus on. You must decide which customers and markets you will pursue, how to promote your products and services to those customers, and what sales methodology you will use to give yourself a competitive advantage in today's market.

Finally, you have to bring your whole team together, explain the entire "plan of battle" to them, and then provide them with all the resources they need to go out and win sales in tough markets.

The Factory Model

This is a concept that you can use in planning and organizing for success as a sales manager. With this method, you view your sales department or sales team as a factory. Just as a factory has raw materials that come in one end and finished products that come out the other end, your sales organization is similar. Your "sales factory" has inputs that include your trained and competent salespeople; money for advertising, promotion, and incentives; desks, chairs, and other resources to support your sales staff; and products and services to sell.

Inside the sales organization, like a factory, certain processes take place. The purpose of these processes is to produce sales results. The job of your salespeople is to use all of the resources or raw materials that you make available and translate them into sales in the current market.

Create Value

The two primary activities of a sales manager are first, to create value, and second, to generate revenues. You should spend 80 percent of your time creating value and generating revenue, all day long.

Almost everything else you do, including and especially dealing with email, social media, messages, and phone calls, are diversions or distractions taking you away from creating value and generating revenue. In the final analysis, your ability to get sales results will be the single most important determinant of your success.

ACTION EXERCISES

1. What specific results are expected of you in your position as sales manager?

2. Of all these results, what is the one result that is most important for you to accomplish, right now?

Build a Great Sales Team

ALL WORK IS done by teams. Your job is essentially that of a team builder and a team leader. All teams depend on the peak performance of each team member. Your job is to assemble a superior team first, then to bring every member on the team up to top performance. Your goal is to build the best sales organization you can and to win in competitive markets.

Top Sports Teams

A sales team is like a sports team in many important respects. By applying the same principles that top sports coaches apply to win championships in their leagues, you can build a championship sales team as well. Top sports teams exhibit six key winning characteristics.

1. CLEAR COACHING AND LEADERSHIP

On a top team, everyone knows who the boss is. This is the person who "calls the shots." Of course, democratic and participatory management are essential for building and maintaining high levels of motivation and morale. But for a crack sales team to perform well, everyone has to know who the coach is. As the sales manager, you are the one in charge. You are the person who sets the standards and calls the plays. Too much democracy does not seem to work in running a sales team against tough competition in a difficult market.

2. COMMITMENT TO EXCELLENCE

As Vince Lombardi said, "Winning is not everything, but wanting to win is."

Top sports teams, like top sales teams, are on the field to win—to achieve high levels of sales and outperform their competition in the market. They are not working just to get through the day. Top salespeople, like top sportsmen and sportswomen, want to win championships and get the bonus money, prizes, and rewards that go along with success.

Perhaps the best motivator of all, in sales or in sports, is the desire and determination to "be the best." Unfortunately, if you do not make a clear spoken commitment to be the best with your salespeople and your team, you will unwittingly slip down into mediocrity. If you do not decide to be in the top 10 percent or 20 percent of your industry, you will automatically end up in the bottom 80 percent. Only a commitment to excellence motivates people to give their very best to their jobs, in sales or in sports.

3. OPEN COMMUNICATION

In top sports teams, there are no games and no politics among the players. Everybody tells everyone else what they think, all the time. There are no secrets, no sulking, and no hidden agendas. There is no game playing behind closed doors, and no politics or manipulation. In a top sales team, information flows up and down continually, with an open-door policy on your part. You make it clear that you are completely transparent. If people have any questions, they can come to you directly and you will answer them straightforwardly and honestly.

Psychologically, to perform at their best, people need to be able to talk to their bosses, to ask questions, and to get feedback. Top players need to feel that they can express their concerns to their managers without fear of disapproval or criticism.

4. INTENSIVE PEOPLE-DEVELOPMENT FOCUS

Top teams focus intensely on training their players continually, day in and day out. They are always helping people play better at the sport. It is the same with excellent sales managers. They always encourage their people to improve. Top sales managers insist on continuous personal and professional growth and development.

The sales training budget is key to people development. *Sales & Marketing Management* magazine did a study into the sales training practices and budgets of the top 20 percent of profitable companies in every industry. What they discovered was quite surprising. The best companies train new salespeople for six to twelve weeks, and often more, before they put them into the field. Thereafter, they invest an average of $6,000 per year per salesperson in ongoing training.

What top companies and top sales managers have discovered is that the return on investment (ROI) from sales training is ten, twenty, and thirty times greater than the amount they invest. The more money they pour into sales training, the higher their sales and profitability.

5. SELECTIVE PLAYER ASSIGNMENTS

On excellent teams, people are assigned to a position where they can make the greatest contribution to the overall success of the team, based on their special talents and abilities. In sales management, some of your people will be best at selling one product or service and some will do better with other products or services. Some salespeople are excellent in going out and finding new business, while other salespeople are equally excellent in maintaining customer accounts and upselling existing customers into purchasing more and more of your products or services.

The best coaches on a sports team move their players around to find the positions where they can perform at their best. Your job is to move your salespeople around so that they are working in the right jobs, selling the right products and services, to the right kinds of customers for them, so they can perform at their best as well.

6. A HEAVY EMPHASIS ON STRATEGY AND PLANNING

One of the most important things that you can do, and that nobody else can do, is to plan for the activities and sales results of your team. Sit down each day and think about what you could change, improve, or do differently. What have you learned recently, and what actions could you take to improve individual or team performance?

To quote Vince Lombardi again, "To build a championship team, you must become brilliant on the basics."

Your job is to build a team that is brilliant on the basics. The good news is that the better reputation your sales team has for being well trained, and the better sales results they get, the easier it is for you to attract more and better people.

Remember our old friend the "Pareto principle," the 80/20 rule. It says that 20 percent of your activities account for 80 percent of your results. The very best sales managers think continually about the 20 percent of the basics of building a winning team that make all the difference.

ACTION EXERCISES

1. Think of yourself as the general of an army in combat, determined to win against a determined enemy (your competition). What is your plan of battle?

2. What specific resources and training does your team need to win against your competitors? How can you provide these resources to them?

THREE

Select Champions

RECRUITMENT IS the starting point in building a superior sales team. Most problems experienced by sales managers originate in the recruitment of inappropriate people for sales positions in the first place. Selection of the proper salespeople is one of the most difficult tasks you have, but it can account for as much as 90 percent of the success of your sales organization. You therefore need an established selection procedure.

Select Slowly
As Peter Drucker said, "Fast people decisions are almost invariably wrong people decisions." If you select in haste, you will repent at leisure. Take your time.

Poor selection is very expensive. It costs you time, money, aggravation, and the sales that you didn't get because you hired the wrong person.

Proper selection begins with your thinking through the requirements of the job and writing them down. Think on paper. Go into every recruitment interview with a series of written guidelines that you refer to during the interview and selection process.

Define the Exact Results That You Want

Make a list of what the salesperson will be expected to do, day in and day out, and what sales results the salesperson will be expected to achieve and when. It is amazing how many salespeople are recruited with a confused idea of what the company expects them to do. They then become angry and frustrated. The sales manager becomes angry as well and begins to question his own ability.

Some time ago, I worked with a personnel selection and training company that had just hired a successful, experienced saleswoman. In keeping with their profession, the company's recruiters had put her through a battery of personality tests and profiles to be absolutely sure that she would be the right candidate. She passed all the tests with flying colors except for one weakness: She was abnormally low in the category of "personal initiative."

Because she had a stellar track record working for a personnel placement company, my friends decided to hire her anyway. But they had neglected to tell her one important part of the job—that she would be responsible for generating her own leads, making her own appointments, and developing her own client base.

The morning that she began work, her first question was, "Where are my leads?" When she found that she would be responsible for generating her own leads, she was shocked. She almost immediately began to fall apart. By the end of the week, they realized they had made a major mistake and let her go. Lesson learned.

One of the most helpful exercises that I have taught to my clients worldwide is to take a sheet of paper and write out a description of the perfect salesperson or candidate for you and your company. Imagine that there is a Perfect Salesperson Factory and that your sheet of paper is an order form. Once you complete this order form, you can confidently send it to the factory and the factory will send you back the exact person you have described on paper.

Look at Previous Achievement

The greatest single predictor of future performance is past performance. What you are looking for, more than anything else, is someone who has already been successful at the type of job that you are hiring this new person to do.

Ask candidates about their previous performance history. What jobs have they had and how well did they do at those jobs? What was the nature of the business? Was it a tough, competitive sales environment, or was the person selling during a boom time, when there were more buyers than sellers?

Hire for Personality

A famous executive once said, "We don't hire people and train them to be nice; we just hire nice people."

The fact is that people don't change. What you see is what you get. Hiring on the basis of attitude and personality will bring you the best recruitment success. Aptitude is important, but it can often be developed with good training and coaching. But when people have the right attitude and personality, and the necessary amount of energy and ambition, you can teach them what they need to know to be successful in selling. Only hire people who you personally like and enjoy; only hire people who have positive, warm personalities and who are generally cheerful and happy.

The Law of Three

This method will allow you to improve your hiring ability to the 90 percent level. It is a technique that I developed over the years and have taught to many thousands of executives. Some top people in major corporations have told me that it transformed their hiring practices throughout the organization.

When you need a new salesperson, you first interview at least three people for the job before you make any decision at all. If you pay well enough, you'll have plenty of candidates to choose from, not just anyone who will take the job.

The second part of the Law of Three is to interview the candidate that you like at least three *times*. Never, never, never hire a person who you have interviewed only once. It is too easy to be caught up in the emotion of talking, laughing, and interacting with a positive prospective salesperson. It can cloud your judgment.

Three Places, Three People

The third part of the Law of Three is to interview the candidate in three different places. Most people have what I call the "chameleon syndrome." This means that as you move them around, from your office to another office down the hallway, or to a coffee shop across the street, they take on different coloring. They actually change their behavior and personality.

The fourth part of the Law of Three is to have the candidate that you like interviewed by at least three *other people* in your company. Hewlett-Packard has a hiring policy that involves four different managers and at least seven different interviews. At the end of the process, they come together and vote. If any one of them is not convinced that the interviewee would be a good employee, the selection process is terminated and the candidate rejected.

The final part of the Law of Three is for you to interview at least three *references* or people that the candidate has worked with in the past. A great question you can ask the candidate is, "I am going to personally phone each of the references that you have provided. Is there anything that I should know before I call and speak to these people?"

You will often be amazed at what people will tell you when you ask that question.

Remember, the more time that you put in at the beginning, the more time you will save in teaching, training, managing, motivating, and coaching after the salesperson begins working for you. Take your time. Go slowly.

ACTION EXERCISES

1. Make a list, like an order form, describing the ideal salesperson for you and your company. Compare each new candidate against this list.

2. Practice the Law of Three with the next candidate you interview for a sales job, and then practice it continually for the rest of your career.

FOUR

Start Them Off Right

YOU HAVE HEARD the saying, "Well begun is half done."

This idea applies very much to new salespeople. Once you have selected them and taken them on board, take care to start them on a solid foundation, from the very first day.

In studying the performance of thousands of salespeople over the years, one of the important discoveries I have made is that the way the person starts the job is going to determine that person's performance not only in the first weeks and months, but even five and ten years later. In fact, long-term performance for salespeople is largely determined by what happens to them in the first ninety days.

Salespeople can join you with either high, medium, or low sales skills and experience. But even if they have been in sales for several years, when they start with you, you must treat them as if they are brand-new. Just because they have considerable experience at selling other products for other companies does not mean that they know anything about your business, your products, your unique selling features, or your customers. They have what is called "low task-relevant maturity."

Product Knowledge

Fully 70 percent of sales organizations in America do no sales training at all. Instead, they only do "product training." They give the salesperson piles of sales materials, brochures, and product information to read and ingest. They then send them out to make calls, assuming that if they understand the product, they can sell it to critical and demanding customers.

Product knowledge is important. Each salesperson must know the product cold and be able to pass an examination on it. Good product knowledge has two advantages: First, it raises the sales team's confidence and makes it much more likely your salespeople will continue in this job. Second, it raises their credibility when they talk with their prospects.

Sales Skills

Another essential factor for success is excellent sales skills. Some companies spend two to six months training new salespeople before allowing them out on the street to represent the company. IBM invests eighteen months in solid training, half in the classroom and half out in the field with other salespeople, before allowing a salesperson to be alone with a customer for the first time.

Go slowly when you train new salespeople, and never assume that the new salesperson has mastered all the essential skills. There is a rule that says, "Your weakest important skill sets the height of your sales." A new salesperson can be excellent at six out of seven key selling skills, but weakness in the seventh skill will hold that salesperson back from achieving full potential.

A Sales Story

A new salesperson hired by one of my client companies wasn't working out. The company thought it had found the right person. But even after extensive training, he was not selling. Instead of firing him, the company decided to have sales managers accompany him on his sales calls to observe his performance.

It soon became abundantly clear that he was lacking in one key skill area. He was unable to answer specific objections and turn them into reasons for buying.

They took him back into the office and worked with him intensively for eight hours, grilling him on the most common objections a person was likely to hear, and then helping him to answer and overcome those objections smoothly and confidently.

Then they sent him back into the field. Within a month, he was a star, and within three months he was a superstar—the highest-performing salesperson for this company in the country. They had been on the verge of letting him go when they realized that he might be lacking in one single skill. I share this story because it can happen to you with your salespeople and your sales organization as well.

Inspect What You Expect

After you have made all the investment in hiring and training new salespeople, you should commit to supervising them continually until they reach the levels and standards of performance that you have set for them. Monitor their performance regularly, even on a daily basis. Give and get feedback regularly from them. Give them guidance and encouragement in the early days to be sure that you have started them out right.

Some years ago, I took over a sales organization that had twenty-eight salespeople and was completely *demoralized*. The sales from this group were very low. They all worked on straight commission, so if they did not make sales, they did not eat. When I took over, I gave each of them a small stack of three-by-five-inch index cards each morning. Their job was to return at the end of the day with five cards filled out with the name of a prospect they had called on and the results of that call.

Within a week, a miracle took place. Of the twenty-eight salespeople, ten had quit. These were the same people who, as it turned out, were not really making any calls during the day.

The remaining eighteen, however, began to call on five or more new customers each day. Because of the Law of Probability, they began to make sales and collect commissions. Within a week, the sales force was motivated and full of energy again.

Pay Them Quickly

Here is another technique you can use to motivate your salespeople. Pay your new salespeople their commissions on a *daily* basis. It is amazing how motivating it is to come back with a sales order and receive your sales commission immediately.

Follow this policy for the first two to four weeks. After that, pay them their sales commissions every Wednesday and Friday. After that, pay them every Friday. You can often turn a person or an entire sales team around with immediate payment of commissions as soon as they have made the sale. After a time, put them onto a regular twice per month commission schedule, as is typical.

Start Them Well

The more time, effort, and thought you put into starting each salesperson off with excellent product and sales training, the more successful that salesperson will be, and the longer the person will stay with your organization.

ACTION EXERCISES

1. Select one technique to manage and motivate your salespeople, such as holding a short sales meeting at the beginning of each day, and practice it immediately.

2. Make a list of the steps that you are going to follow to ensure that each new salesperson starts fully prepared to be successful.

FIVE

Manage by Sales Objectives

THERE ARE SPECIFIC management techniques you can use to build top salespeople and top sales teams. In business, one of these techniques is called management by objectives. In sales, we call it "management by sales objectives."

The Economist reported on a performance study embracing 10,000 organizations in twenty countries involving about 150 researchers whose goal was to determine the most important predictors of high performance and productivity improvement. What they found was that there were three essential factors that predicted productivity and profitability in competitive markets. These three were setting targets, measuring results, and rewarding performance.

The Big Three

Top sales organizations set clear sales targets and quotas for each salesperson, for each week and month. They set specific action targets for each day. All salespeople know exactly what they are expected to do, day in and day out, from the time they start work until the time they finish.

The second driver of high performance was having clear measures and deadlines for the performance of each task leading to the sale. Salespeople knew exactly how they would be measured, how they would be paid, and the exact timelines and deadlines on which they would be judged.

The third key factor that drove performance was excellent rewards for high performance. The greater clarity that salespeople had with regard to how much more money they could earn if they achieved higher sales goals, the more likely it was that they would achieve those goals.

Manage Them the Same

Sometimes people say to me, "My people all work on straight commission. How can I tell them what to do? Can I set quotas and deadlines for them?"

The fact is that you must manage straight commission and straight salary salespeople using these exact same principles. My friend Jim Rohn used to say that "top people go where the standards are the highest."

If you want to attract and keep good people, treat them like a crack team, with clear standards and disciplines that you insist on every single day. Impose clear controls on everything that they do and help them measure up to the agreed-on standards. The very best salespeople perform at the highest levels when they are working in a tightly organized, well-disciplined sales team.

Manage Them Differently

Salespeople have different levels of experience and ability. New salespeople should have sales quotas and goals that are commensurate with their knowledge and experience. More experienced, successful salespeople should have higher sales quotas. Sit down with each member of your team and determine the correct sales quotas for that salesperson, based on the individual's background and the current market. Clarify the activities the salesperson must do each day.

Define the sales goals in terms of the daily activities necessary to achieve them. Establish clear measures of performance. Remember: What gets measured gets done.

In sales, you cannot control or determine where the next sale is going to come from. You can only control the daily activities of the salesperson, which will ultimately determine the number of sales that take place in any market. Although you cannot control the sales in the short term, you can control the activities that inevitably lead to those sales.

Tell Them What to Do

Make it clear that each salesperson is expected to make a specific number of customer calls each day. All salespeople are expected to follow up and meet with prospective customers face-to-face. They are expected to call back prospects that they have called on recently, as well as existing customers.

They are expected to send out a specific number of emails or letters, have a specific number of interviews, and so on.

If telephone prospecting is the key to getting appointments, set a minimum standard of ten telephone contacts by 11:00 a.m. each morning. When people come to work, they take their call sheets, sit down, and begin telephoning immediately. Your job is to make sure that each salesperson is doing his or her job, as agreed upon.

There is nothing that motivates a salesperson more than to have a clear, specific track to run on. On the other hand, there is nothing that demoralizes or demotivates a salesperson faster than coming into work and rattling around like a marble in a can, with no clear direction or specific activities required.

Discuss and Agree

With new salespeople, sit down and discuss and agree on the specific activities that they will engage in each day. At the end of each day, have a brief review with them, on paper, to make sure that they are fulfilling their commitments. After a salesperson has done this review for a while and begins to make sales and earn commissions, you can let off the pressure and check on the person once or twice a week. But at the beginning, have your new salespeople report to you every day. You know the rule: Inspect what you expect. Make sure that all of your salespeople know that you are going to be checking on them on a regular basis. Then, be consistent and persistent in measuring both sales results and activities.

Ken Blanchard says, "Feedback is the breakfast of champions." One of your jobs is to give good counseling and reviews of performance each day. Discuss with your sales team what they have done, how it worked out, and how they feel about their experience. What did they learn?

Two Magic Questions

There are two questions that you should ask of a salesperson at the end of a call or at the end of the day. The first magic question is, "What did you do right?"

This is a *positive* question. You are encouraging your salespeople to review the entire procedure from the time they picked up the phone to call and make the appointment, through preparation, arriving at the appointment, making the presentation, and everything that took place in the sales meeting.

Aristotle once wrote that "wisdom is an equal measure of experience plus reflection." When you help your salespeople to reflect on what they did right—the positive aspects of their sales work—you reinforce and drive the memory of these positive actions deeper into their subconscious minds. As a result, they will remember to replay and repeat these behaviors in their subsequent sales calls.

The second magic question is, "What would you do differently next time?"

The answer to this question is also positive. It helps salespeople to review their own performance and think of ways that they could improve "next time."

Old-school sales managers would often grill their sales-people by asking them, "What did you do wrong? Where did you screw up? How did you blow the sale?" But psychologists have found that when you review the negative aspects of a person's behavior, it is those negative aspects that are recorded and reinforced in the subconscious mind, making them much more likely to reappear in the next sales call.

On the other hand, when you talk to people about what they did *right*, and what they would do differently next time, they are much more likely to improve their performance—and far more rapidly than you might imagine.

A Sense of Mastery

One of the greatest of all motivations is the feeling of personal empowerment through learning and growth. People love to feel that they are developing a sense of mastery in their careers. When you help them think about how they could perform even better in the future, they feel happy about themselves, happy about you, and happy about the job.

ACTION EXERCISES

1. Develop and discuss clear goals and objectives for sales and sales activities for each salesperson who reports to you.

2. Arrange to meet regularly with each salesperson, or with the group in a sales meeting, to review and both get and give feedback on activities and results.

SIX

The Psychology of Sales Success

PERHAPS THE greatest discovery in psychology in the twentieth century was the discovery of the self-concept. It turns out that there is a direct relationship between the self-concept of the salesperson (i.e., what the salesperson thinks, feels, and believes about himself) and the person's level of sales performance.

People sell effectively to the exact degree to which they consider themselves to be good at selling. Top salespeople not only like to sell, but they consider themselves to be excellent at the profession of selling. As the result of this self-concept, they sell vastly more than those who may doubt themselves and their ability.

Multiple Self-Concepts

People also have a self-concept for how much money they earn. People cannot earn more than 10 percent above or below their self-concept level of income without engaging in *compensating* behaviors. If they earn 10 percent or more than they feel themselves capable of, they engage in "throwaway actions." They spend their money on frivolous things, give or gamble it away, and even engage in harmful personal behaviors.

If they earn 10 percent *below* their self-concept of level of income, they engage in "scrambling" behaviors. They work harder, they put in more hours, they talk to more people, they become more aggressive about earning, and they do everything possible to get their income back up into their self-concept range of income.

Performance Improvement

All improvements in performance on the *outside* begin with improvements in the self-concept—the way we think and feel about ourselves on the *inside*. You can have a great influence on your sales team's performance improvement as the sales manager.

One of your main jobs as a sales manager is to do everything possible to boost the salesperson's self-concept as a top performer. Human beings are inordinately influenced by the authority figures in their environment: their parents, their bosses, and other important people. As a result, you are the most important *external* influence on self-concept in the salesperson's life.

There are three parts of the self-concept that you need to be aware of: the self-ideal, self-image, and self-esteem. Everything you do to improve your salespeople's self-concept in one or more of these areas improves their performance, their sales, and their results.

The Self-Ideal

This is a combined picture or vision of the very best person that the salesperson could possibly be. The self-ideal is made up of the goals, aspirations, and most admired and desired virtues and qualities of the salesperson. The greater clarity that someone has regarding the very best person he or she could possibly be, the faster the person moves toward becoming that person. The self-ideal has an inordinate influence on feelings and behavior.

To raise the self-ideal of salespeople, you encourage them to select the very best people in your industry as their role models or standards. Refer to the top people in your company, department, or even people from other industries and say, "This is the kind of person you can be. If you work hard, learn and practice the right things, and persist, you too can be one of the best people in the business."

BE A ROLE MODEL

In improving the salesperson's self-ideal, remember that this individual is greatly influenced by your position as a role model. As a rule, if you want to have better salespeople, you must become a better sales manager.

The quality of your people, your sales team, will usually be a *reflection* of your personal qualities, characteristics, and abilities. When your salespeople like you, respect you, and admire you, they will strive to be more and more like you. Continually ask yourself, "What kind of a company would my company be if everyone in it was just like me?"

The Self-Image

Your self-image determines your performance minute to minute, day to day. This is often called your "inner mirror." It is what you look into before each upcoming event or situation to see how you are supposed to behave. Your self-image then determines what you do and how you perform.

Your self-image is determined by three factors. The first is the way that you see yourself in comparison to your ideal self. The more you feel that you are performing at your best—that is, as the best salesperson you could possibly be—the more positive your self-image will be, the more competent you become, and the more your sales performance improves.

WHAT YOU THINK

The second component of your self-image is how you think that you are viewed, seen, or talked about by other people. We are inordinately influenced by the opinions other people have of us. When you continually compliment and praise your salespeople, they see themselves as better and more competent, and that is how they perform when they are with a customer.

The third factor that determines self-image is how people *think* that other people are thinking about them. If a person feels admired and respected, especially by his or her manager, that person will perform well out in the field away from the office.

STARTING ANEW

The good news is that whenever people start a new job, they have an opportunity to develop a new self-image for how they perform at that job. This self-image is determined from the first minute of the first hour by how they are treated by the people in their work environment, especially the boss. When you express welcome, appreciation, and confidence in your new salespeople, they will often amaze you with how good they become and how fast they become sales superstars.

The Self-Esteem

The third part of the self-concept is self-esteem. This is easily the most important part of your personality. It is the control valve on sales performance and is determined by how people feel about themselves, by their *emotions*.

There seems to be a direct relationship between people's level of self-esteem, "how much they like themselves," and their sales performance. Everything that you do or say to cause people to like and respect themselves more increases their sense of personal value, enthusiasm, and determination when they are in the field dealing with customers.

One of your main jobs as a sales manager is to make people feel important and valuable. Everything that you do or say that makes your people feel more important or more valuable will boost their self-esteem, improve their self-image, and motivate them to perform even better.

MAKE PEOPLE FEEL LIKE WINNERS

Perhaps the most influential factor in raising self-esteem in others and causing them to feel like "winners" is success experiences—that is, actually *making sales*. Everything that you do to teach, train, manage, and motivate your people to actually make sales, and make more money, causes their self-esteem to go up. And the higher their self-esteem, the more likely it is they will make even more sales.

ACTION EXERCISES

1. Become a sales psychologist to your people, continually looking for ways to improve their performance by building up their self-concepts and self-esteem.

2. From now on, see yourself as responsible for making your people feel like winners; open every conversation with praise, approval, or encouragement.

SEVEN

Practice the Performance Formula

EACH PERSON behaves at a certain level today and can behave at a higher level in the future. The performance formula is A × M = P (ability times motivation equals performance). It is your attitude more than your aptitude that determines your *altitude*.

Ability is a function of aptitude, the necessary characteristics and qualities required for a particular job, plus experience, plus training, plus education.

Aptitude itself is a function of three factors: First, it is a function of natural ability, which can be inborn or can be developed. Second, it is a function of experience. The more relevant experience people have (or have had) in performing the sales or sales management function, the better they are going to be. Third, aptitude is greatly affected by training.

Accelerate Ability

As a sales manager, you cannot change the natural ability or experience of a salesperson. Those are in the past. Those are the factors that come with the package when you hire or field a salesperson.

However, you can change, modify, or accelerate training, education, and personal development. When you start off with the right people in terms of personality and attitude, you can multiply and accelerate their ability to make a contribution to your company with continuous training and education, like an athlete joining a sports team.

Over the years, I have worked with more than 1,000 large companies in sixty-eight countries. It seems that all successful companies have top sales forces. And all top sales forces, including those of IBM, Xerox, Google, Microsoft, and Hewlett-Packard, spend millions of dollars every year training their people. They have discovered that there is a direct relationship between training and sales success, or success of any other kind.

The Four Factors of Motivation

Motivation is a function of four different factors: leadership, organizational climate, rewards, and individual needs. You can influence each one of these to a greater or lesser degree. The first is leadership style. The most important person on the sales team is the sales manager. Sales managers can affect the motivation and performance of everyone who reports to them. Your leadership ability—your ability to inspire, empower, and encourage people—is a powerful factor in motivation and performance. As the IBM executives discovered, the sales manager is the "pivotal skill" in the organization. Changing the sales manager or improving this manager's performance can lead to a dramatic and almost immediate increase in sales results.

A Great Place to Work

The second factor in motivation is the organizational climate. Is your company a great place to work? Are people happy, positive, and cheerful? Do people get along well with each other and look forward to coming to work? Do they feel that they can express themselves and their concerns openly and honestly to their boss?

There is a simple way to determine if you have created a great place to work. It is called the "laugh test." Because laughter occurs spontaneously and unplanned, it is always a true test of the quality of the relationships among any group of people.

In a good company, people laugh a lot. They tell a lot of jokes and joke around with each other. They are always smiling and cheerful. They are obviously happy to be at their place of work. And the more people laugh at work, the more confident and positive they feel, and the more they will sell.

The Reward Structure

The third factor affecting attitude is the reward structure. As Khrushchev said, "Call it what you will, but people are motivated by incentives."

It turns out that salespeople have two major motivators: *money and status*. They are motivated by earning more money and the potential to earn more money. This drives the most ambitious and highest-performing salespeople more than any other single factor.

They are also motivated by status, by being made to feel important in the company. But never make the mistake of thinking that you can replace giving people more money with status rewards, like trophies and plaques.

Money as the Motivator

Many top executives in business have never been in sales. They often think that salespeople are not or should not be motivated by money. They think that salespeople should be motivated by the love of their work or by some feeling of company loyalty. These executives are almost invariably wrong.

During the dot-com boom of the 1990s, the president of a fast-growing Silicon Valley firm, who had never been in sales, announced that effective immediately, all salespeople would be paid exactly the same, regardless of their sales results. He felt that competition among the salespeople to make more sales was "unseemly." Salespeople should get their motivation from some source other than money. This announcement was made in the national press.

What do you think happened? Within six months, all of the firm's top salespeople had left and joined competitive companies that offered them premium rewards for excellent sales results. The only people who stayed were the average or mediocre salespeople who were quite content to have a guaranteed salary. Six months later, the company went broke. The competition ate it alive. To this day, the company can't understand why sales dropped 80 percent in less than a year and all of its investors lost everything.

What People Need

The fourth factor in motivation is the need structure of each individual. Different people at different stages of their sales careers have different needs if they are to perform at their best.

New salespeople need clear structure and supervision. They need to be told exactly what to do and when to do it, and then they need to be supervised carefully to make sure that they do their job, that they do it well, and that they do it on time.

Senior salespeople have different needs. They need largely to be left alone. They want to have a friendly camaraderie with their sales manager and then have the sales manager simply get out of their way so that they can go out and bring in the sales. They very much resent being overcontrolled or having their freedom limited or curtailed for any reason.

Your job as a sales manager is to find out and understand the needs of each salesperson. Some need more guidance. They need to talk to their sales manager on a regular basis. They need regular feedback. They need skills coaching and hand-holding. Others neither need nor want any of these things. They just want to go out and make sales.

Keep asking, "What do my salespeople need to be motivated? What does this particular salesperson need to perform at his/her best?"

In most cases, the answer is simple. They need clear sales goals and objectives; clear, written, and measurable standards of performance and deadlines; sales success experiences; and rewards based on performance. They need praise and encouragement and recognition for a job well done. If you can give them these things, they will go out and make sales in any market.

ACTION EXERCISES

1. Make a list of your salespeople, and next to each name, write one or two specific needs that each individual might have to be more productive.

2. Treat all of your salespeople as if they have the potential to be superstars if you can just create the proper environment in which they can perform at their best.

EIGHT

Improve Your Leadership Style

THE ONE FACTOR that can be changed immediately in the performance formula, and that can bring about almost immediate improvements in performance, is *leadership style*. Everything that you do to improve your own personal leadership abilities will act as a multiplier for your sales force and increase their sales results. The best news is that there are no limits on how much better you can become as a sales manager and a leader when you devote yourself to self-improvement.

Many thousands of employees and salespeople have been asked the question, "Who was the best boss you ever had, and why?" It seems that the best bosses in every field, including sales, have two specific qualities: *clarity* and *consideration*.

In defining *clarity*, the people surveyed said, "I always knew exactly what the sales manager expected me to do." The manager set clear goals and objectives, discussed them in detail with the salespeople, and then helped them to achieve those targets. The salespeople knew, every day, exactly what they were supposed to do, from the time they started work in the morning until the end of the day.

In my experience, clarity is 95 percent of success, not only in business and sales, but in life. The greater clarity you have with regard to what it is that you want to accomplish, and the greater clarity that each person who reports to you has, the faster and easier you will get the results you desire.

Caring About Your People

The second quality of the best bosses was "consideration." People surveyed said, "I always felt as if my boss cared about me as a person, as well as an employee."

In practice, this meant that the boss would take time to ask the sales employees about their personal lives, their families, and how everything was going in their time away from the office. This means that, when you talk about business, you focus on sales results. And when you talk to the individual, you focus on things of a personal nature.

What percentage of people's thinking is emotional, and what percentage is logical/rational? The answer is that people are 100 percent emotional. The fastest way to connect with an individual is to ask something about the person's emotional life: the individual's personal and family life, aside from the job. This immediately triggers feelings of warmth toward the manager and greater commitment and loyalty to the company.

Four Management Styles

You've probably seen the managerial grid that divides management personalities into four different quadrants or styles. These are sometimes called *telling, selling, managing,* and *motivating.*

It is important that you use the right style of management for the particular individual with whom you are working. For example, a new person requires "telling," which is a directive, hands-on style of managing. You tell the person exactly what to do, how to do it, when to do it, and how it will be measured. You then follow up, like a master teaching an apprentice, to make sure that the new salesperson is doing exactly what's required to get the results you expect.

The second type of management is "selling." This is when you take the time to explain to your salespeople what they are doing and why. You encourage and persuade them to do what they need to do to get sales results, both for the company and for themselves.

Managing and Motivating

The third leadership style is "managing." This style is used with experienced salespeople who only need a little direction and guidance to do their jobs. You set clear goals and standards accompanied with clear measures of activity. You then make sure that they are doing what they are expected to do each day.

The fourth leadership style is "motivating." You create an incentive structure within your business that motivates people to perform at ever-higher levels. For example, the most successful companies have regular sales contests of some kind. They can be daily, weekly, and monthly contests. The biggest companies have annual contests whereby salespeople can earn bonuses, prizes, vacations, and financial rewards if they meet and exceed their sales quotas.

One of my clients had a simple reward system. He would take the top-selling salesperson out to lunch to an expensive restaurant on the first day of the following month. The top salespeople, who were earning good incomes already, would not be motivated by a small increase in their income. But being taken out to lunch by the boss was a status symbol, which strongly motivated them.

In the last few days of the month, there would be a flurry of sales activity among the top salespeople, those who were doing 80 percent of the business, just for the honor of walking out the door for lunch with the boss on the first workday of the month.

What kind of motivational incentives could you create within your workplace that would cause people to perform at their very highest levels?

The Golden Rule

Jack Welch told the managers at General Electric, "Always manage your staff as if the situation would be reversed and you would be working for that person one year from today."

General Electric had a high-performance system of incentives and rewards. It was not unusual for top-performing people to be promoted over the heads of their bosses. It happened every year. It was a good idea for each manager to be aware that it could happen to him. As a result, each person was treated with respect.

The Golden Rule says that you lead and guide others the way you would like to be led yourself. Guide them the way you would like to be guided. Give them feedback the way you would like to get feedback. Build them up and encourage them to perform at ever-higher levels as you would like to be encouraged.

In your interactions with each salesperson, you should supervise, counsel, coach, and discipline the individual in the same way that you would like to be treated.

One of the most important parts of Golden Rule management is that you give your salespeople the freedom to perform. People who have worked under exceptional leaders say that one of the things they liked the most was that they had considerable freedom to determine their daily work routine as long as they delivered the sales results expected of them.

Different Strokes for Different Folks

Remember also that each person is different. Each salesperson may require a different style of leadership, or a combination of styles, depending on the person's experience and personal situation at the time. Be prepared to be flexible and to treat each salesperson as a unique individual, different from every other salesperson who reports to you.

ACTION EXERCISES

1. Review a list of the names of the members of your sales team. Write down next to each name the ideal leadership style that you could practice that would help that person perform at higher levels.

2. Practice consideration. Make it a habit each day to ask your salespeople simple questions like, "How is everything going?" Or, "How are you feeling today?" Or, "How is your family?" You will be amazed at the kind of responses that you get from these types of general questions that focus on the person rather than on the job. And the more you ask these questions, the more loyal and committed your salespeople will be, both to you and to the company.

NINE

Reward Sales Performance

IN LIFE, BUSINESS, and sales, everyone wants to feel like a winner. How do you get the winning feeling? Simple. You win and you get rewarded for your win!

Whenever you accomplish a goal or achieve something worthwhile, such as making a sale or hitting your quota, you feel as if you have just crossed the finish line. You feel like a winner. Each time you succeed, your self-esteem and self-confidence go up. You feel great about yourself. That feeling is perhaps the greatest reward of all.

There are other rewards for winners.

Money Motivates

The most obvious reward is money. Money connected to achievement makes people feel happy and successful.

Earning lots of money based on your own efforts is a perpetual source of drive and enthusiasm. Money is meaningful because it can buy cars, clothes, better homes and apartments, status items, and an enhanced lifestyle.

Whenever business owners or sales managers ask me how they can motivate their people without giving them more money, I tell them that I have no idea. Salespeople think about how much money they are earning, how much they have, and how much their lifestyle costs all the time.

Make People Feel Important

Another major reward is *status*. Everything that you can do to raise the status and prestige of your salespeople as the result of their making sales motivates them to make even more sales in the future.

Every year, the best companies present prizes, awards, certificates, trophies, plaques, and other awards to their highest-performing salespeople. They usually present them in large meetings and award ceremonies so that others can see the winners and be motivated to be up on that stage themselves sometime in the future.

It turns out that the *faster* you acknowledge an accomplishment, the greater will be the boost in self-esteem and self-confidence, and the more likely it is that that behavior will be repeated. So, when someone makes a sale, you should make a big thing of it right away. You should thank your salespeople, congratulate them, shake their hands, and express your appreciation and admiration for their accomplishment that very day.

Brag About Them

A powerful way to reward people for higher achievement, and to build their status, is to brag about them to other people, in their presence. When one of your salespeople makes a good sale or gets through to a difficult prospect, you should take that person to the "big boss" in your company and tell the senior executive what a wonderful job this person has done and how he or she did it.

When you stand there bragging about your employee to someone else, while the salesperson stands right there and listens, that employee will feel even more valuable and important—and more motivated to repeat the behavior that you are praising him for.

Recognition is another powerful motivating influence. They say that athletes, especially runners, perform at their best and break records more often in front of large audiences rather than small audiences. There's something about the applause of a huge crowd that causes athletes to perform beyond anything they've ever done before. Most records for most athletic events are broken during the Olympics, when millions of people are watching.

Look for ways to recognize, reward, praise, and encourage sales performance, and whenever possible, do these things immediately after the sales result has been achieved. The faster that you recognize and reward people for their performance, the more likely it is that they will repeat that performance.

Pay Attention to Others

An effective way of rewarding sales performance is through *attention*. Personal attention by the manager and other top people in the company is a big motivator. We always pay attention to people who we most value. The more attention that you lavish on people for achieving sales results, the more valuable and important they feel. Their self-esteem and self-confidence go up. They are motivated to repeat the performance.

How do you give people the gift of attention? You spend time with your top salespeople. This is a valuable use of your time, far more important than paperwork. Whenever you have a choice of spending time with one of your salespeople or taking care of busywork, choose the salesperson. The other work can wait.

The rule is to spend individual time with your top performers and group time with your average performers. Top performers highly value one-on-one face time with their bosses. This is considered to be a reward that they will strive to earn by hitting ever-higher sales targets.

Offer Promotion and Advancement

Promotion or advancement to a more responsible position is a major motivator for salespeople. It makes them feel special and important. They feel more like winners. Any suggestion or opportunity that you can use to help your people move up the corporate ladder is a powerful motivator.

Many salespeople hope to advance into sales supervision and sales management in the future. But be careful. Most excellent salespeople are not good managers, and advancing a salesperson into management can actually be harmful to the individual and to the company. You can lose a good salesperson and acquire a poor manager—a double detriment.

But there is something else that you can do. You can have different rankings of salespeople such as Sales Consultant, then moving up to Sales Associate, then moving up to Sales Executive or Senior Sales Executive. You can promote salespeople up through the sales ranks.

You can create a range of titles, like in the military, that people can aspire to, and have their new titles printed on their business cards as they achieve certain sales goals in their careers. This can act as a powerful motivator for increased sales activity and sales success.

ACTION EXERCISES

1. Identify your top salespeople, the top 20 percent who do 80 percent of the business, and decide on one behavior or action you are going to practice to personally recognize and acknowledge them, preferably in front of others. Whatever you decide, put it into practice immediately.

2. Think about your average or problem salespeople and determine one behavior that you can practice that might help them move ahead and motivate them to perform at higher levels. Whatever your decision, do it immediately.

TEN

Develop Winning Salespeople

THE STARTING POINT of building a top team of excellent salespeople is to carefully recruit them in the first place. Generally speaking, people don't change. This is why 95 percent of your success as a sales manager will be determined by your selection process in the first place.

The second key to motivating excellent people is continuous training and development. It is not possible for your sales team to achieve peak performance without continual training, just as it would not be possible to field a winning sports team without training them continually.

Achieve Sales Fitness

If you were a coach responsible for training athletes to perform in the Olympics, you would be directing their training and development every day. Just as you require regular physical exercise to attain and maintain high levels of physical fitness, you require continual levels of training and development to maintain high levels of sales fitness.

The highest-performing sales organizations are those that train every week or even every day. Many sales managers and company owners from my seminars have told me that, as a result of daily training, they were able to increase the sales of their companies by 200 percent, 300 percent, and even 500 percent in a single year. They almost always admit that they were astonished at the improvement in sales results they achieved when they began a regular training program for their salespeople.

Develop Personal Learning Programs

It may be that your schedule does not allow for daily sales training of your entire team. In this case, you can lay out a personal and professional development program for each salesperson. You should have a chart or a list that lays out the subjects that your salespeople need to acquire and the activities your salespeople are going to engage in to develop these skills. This list should include audiobooks that they can listen to as they travel to sales meetings with customers. You should recommend books and articles for them to read. Your list can include online videos that they can watch in the morning before they start work.

You should have an internal sales training program that new sales employees are required to attend when they begin, and an ongoing sales training program that is mandatory for all of your salespeople on at least a weekly basis.

Engage in Weekly Sales Training

One of my clients, the sales manager of a division of a multinational company, told me that he started a weekly sales training program that consisted of playing one sales video per week, followed by discussion. Within one year, this division was turning in the highest levels of sales and profitability in the worldwide organization.

He said that the day after the sales training day was the highest sales day of the week. By training salespeople for one hour per week, and then discussing how they were going to use what they had learned when they went out to talk to customers, the whole organization increased its sales to the highest levels ever experienced.

The Basic Rule for Performance

There is a basic rule in business and in sales: You cannot expect people to get a specific result if you have not trained them thoroughly in exactly what they need to do to achieve that result. Sometimes a single technique that has been tested and proved can help a person get more appointments, or make more effective presentations, or close more sales.

The additional benefit of developing an ongoing sales training program for your people is that it helps them make more sales and make more money. It soon becomes known in the market that, if you want to make more money in this field, the best thing you can do is join this sales organization because it provides the best training in the industry.

One thing that salespeople like, as much or more than anything else, is to be trained to earn more money and to become more valuable. Salespeople think a lot about their "earning ability" and are always looking for ways to increase it.

ACTION EXERCISES

1. Make a list of the seven essential sales skills that each person must have to be successful: prospecting, building trust and rapport, identifying needs accurately, presenting persuasively, answering objections effectively, closing the sale, and getting resales and referrals (see Chapter 14). Next, on a scale of one to ten, evaluate how well trained each of your salespeople is in each of these key skill areas.

2. Sit down with each salesperson and develop a personal and professional growth plan with and for the individual. Encourage your salespeople to be learning and growing every day in some way as a regular part of their sales and work activities.

ELEVEN

Plan Sales Activities

THE 80/20 RULE applies to all areas of life, especially in all areas of sales. The fact is that only 20 percent of salespeople are genuinely proactive. They can "plan their work and work their plan."

Fully 80 percent of salespeople need a track to run on. They need clear and specific direction, with goals, measures, deadlines, and standards. This is an important part of your job as a sales manager.

Control the Controllable

For countless reasons, it is very difficult to determine exactly who your next customer is going to be. You cannot control whether people buy now, buy later, or decline to buy at all.

There are too many external factors in the life and work of the potential customer to make accurate predictions.

But you can control sales activities on an hour-by-hour and day-to-day basis. By controlling the sales *activities*, you can indirectly control the sales results.

The Law of Probability says that if you engage in more activities aimed at generating sales, you will ultimately generate more sales. One of the fastest ways to increase sales results is to increase sales activity. Prospect more often, call on more people, see more people, call back more often, and respond to more requests for information. The higher the level of sales activity, the higher the level of sales, even though you cannot predict exactly where they will come from.

There is a direct relationship between the number of prospective customers that a salesperson contacts, calls on, visits, or emails and the number of sales the salesperson will make. One of the fastest ways to increase your sales is to specify the number of calls that each person is required to make each day. This is the simplest control of all, easy to calculate and easy to measure.

If all you do is require a certain number of calls, and then record and review those calls each day, your sales will go up.

One of my client companies turned its sales around with a simple policy. Every salesperson was required to make five new calls per day and 100 new calls each month. Since there are twenty-two working days in an average month, this simple measure was quite effective.

The job of the sales manager was to get everyone to agree to this call quota. Then the sales manager would monitor the call reports submitted by the salespeople on a daily basis. As soon as salespeople knew that they were going to be graded and evaluated on making a minimum number of calls, the level of call activity increased dramatically, and so did the sales.

The 100 Call Method

A performance improvement strategy that I teach is the "100 call method." With this method, the company runs a contest for the first person who can make 100 new customer contacts. The beauty of this method is that no sales are required. The job of the salesperson is simply to make contact by telephone and by personal visit with 100 new prospective clients.

When the salespeople are required to make these contacts, but are under no pressure to make sales, they relax and surprisingly become more effective. Because they both *care and don't care*, they make more calls, and more and more of those calls turn into customers.

Pair Them Up

You can pair up your salespeople and have a simple contest. The first person to make 100 calls in the pair or group is taken out for lunch by the other person or members of the group. As the sales manager, you can give a gift certificate for dinner at a nice restaurant for the salesperson and his or her spouse as a reward for making 100 calls before anyone else.

Every individual and organization who has ever installed this 100 call method is absolutely amazed at the immediate increases in sales. Even more amazing is the increase in morale. Everybody becomes more positive, enthusiastic, and less reluctant to keep on making calls after the contest period has ended.

The Thank-You Card Method

One organization I worked with installed a simple system. Employees had to come back to the office at the end of the day and send out ten thank-you cards to people they had contacted or met with that day. The company provided the cards, the envelopes, and paid for the postage.

The special power of this method was that company salespeople had to come back to the office at the end of the day with the names and addresses of at least ten people they had called on. They would then sit with their coworkers and fill out their cards. The sales manager would collect the thank-you cards and mail them.

Because of this scrutiny and peer pressure, salespeople were highly motivated to come back to the office with ten or more people to whom they could send thank-you cards each day. The sales increased almost immediately, as did the morale of the salespeople.

I worked with one sales organization that was ranked number fifteen out of fifteen company branches in that city. The organization had thirty salespeople. Within thirty days of requiring that each salesperson send out ten thank-you cards each evening, they were down to eighteen salespeople. People who were unwilling to call on enough people simply faded away. No disciplinary discussions or firing interviews were necessary. They just quit on their own.

Meanwhile, the eighteen salespeople who were sending out ten cards per day had driven the branch to number one in sales out of the fifteen branches within ninety days.

Fast Tempo Is Essential

There is a direct relationship between fast tempo and success, especially in sales. In the best sales organizations, everyone is busy and moving quickly all the time. No one is sitting around chatting with coworkers, drinking coffee, or reading the newspaper. People are busy, busy, busy. Your job is to keep your people busy, moving, and active. Keep raising the standards on sales activities. Make them work harder, and harder still. Insist that they work quickly and respond quickly to opportunities, ideas, and customer inquiries. Have them start earlier and work later.

Fast tempo will translate into more contacts, then better contacts, and then very quickly into more sales. The overall level of energy and productivity will go up. People will be happier and more positive. Everyone will make more sales and more money.

Salespeople love to have clear targets to aim at. They love to be busy and active. They love to be working and getting sales results. And the busier you keep them, the more they will like and respect you and see you as a true leader.

ACTION EXERCISES

1. Set clear activity goals for each salesperson. Be sure the goals are written down and checked daily. Tell your salespeople that this exercise is to ensure that they each earn as much money as possible.

2. Organize a "100 calls" contest among your sales team. Create a prize for the winners. Repeat it two to four times per year.

TWELVE

Satisfy Salespeople's Basic Needs

EVERYONE HAS basic needs that must be met before people can perform at their best. One of your jobs as the sales manager is to structure the work so that these needs are satisfied and the salesperson is both psychologically and emotionally free to achieve sales results.

Maslow's Hierarchy

Psychologist Abraham Maslow was famous for his hierarchy of needs, the discovery that each person has five basic needs, each of which has to be satisfied to a certain level before the next need could be satisfied.

The first of these basic needs is the need for *survival*. The survival instinct is the most powerful of all emotions. If physical survival is threatened, we think of nothing else. We lose all interest in the satisfaction of any other needs. Fortunately, in our society, except for rare incidences, survival is largely guaranteed and taken for granted.

The second basic need, once survival is assured, is the need for *safety and security*. By safety and security we mean all kinds of security, such as physical security, emotional security, and especially financial security.

Physical security requires that people have sufficient food, shelter, clothing, transportation, and other basic needs. Emotional security requires that people be liked, accepted, and trusted by the important people around them. Financial security requires that we have enough money so that we are not preoccupied with fear of poverty or loss.

EACH NEED MUST BE SATISFIED

Each of these two basic needs must be satisfied to a certain level (which is different for each person) before the individual can think about satisfying or achieving higher-level needs. This is why financial security, earning enough to be able to maintain a certain lifestyle, is essential to salespeople performing at their best.

THE NEED TO BELONG

The third level of needs identified by Maslow was that of *belongingness*. People need to know and feel that they are recognized and accepted by the people around them, in both their work and social environments.

When someone joins a company, the first thing that happens is that the new employee is introduced to coworkers.

When coworkers recognize, like, and accept one another and work together in a spirit of harmony and cooperation, high morale is created in the organization, which leads to better performance of the work.

In my company, I consider myself to be largely responsible for maintaining harmony and peace. My job is to make sure that everyone else is happy and comfortable in doing their jobs. For this reason, I will quickly remove anyone from my company if I find that the person is a source of negativity of any kind. Since my staff know that I will not allow them to be subjected to the negativity of anyone else, they are much happier and more productive in everything they do.

THE NEED TO BUILD SELF-ESTEEM

The fourth need that people have is for *self-esteem*. People need to feel valuable, important, and respected. People need to feel that they are liked and admired by others. People need to like themselves and consider themselves to be important contributors to the organization.

Everything you do as a sales manager to build self-esteem in your salespeople also builds their self-confidence. This self-confidence then leads to greater sales activity and better sales results.

The highest level in Maslow's hierarchy was considered to be *self-actualization*. This is the feeling that you are fulfilling more and more of your potential, rising steadily to greater heights, and achieving the respect, recognition, and admiration of all the people around you. You are becoming *everything* you are capable of becoming.

One of your goals as sales manager is to help people move through the five levels of the hierarchy of needs, all the way up to self-esteem and self-actualization. People who are dedicated to fulfilling their needs at these higher levels are the happiest, most creative, and highest-performing people on your team.

Three Basic Needs at Work

The three basic needs that people have at work are: *dependence, independence,* and *interdependence.*

DEPENDENCE

Dependence needs are satisfied when people feel that they are a part of something that is bigger than themselves. They are parts of a company or organization. They belong to it, and it belongs to them. This is why the more time you spend telling people what is going on in the company, and including them in discussions and decisions, the more they feel that they are part of the company rather than the company being a separate entity from them.

Robert Reich, former secretary of labor, said that when he walks into a company he can tell immediately the psychological and emotional climate of the people who are working there by the way they refer to themselves and the company. In top companies, he says, people use the words *my, we,* and *our* to describe the business: "This is my company. Our goals in this company are to achieve these results. We work together to accomplish these goals."

INDEPENDENCE

The second need each person has is for independence or autonomy. People need to feel that they stand out and are recognized as individuals, apart from being members of the team. This is why recognition, rewards, and reinforcement of individual performance are important motivators if you want to elicit high performance from your sales team members.

INTERDEPENDENCE

The third and highest need is for interdependence. This is the feeling that we are a vital part of a team that is working toward achieving important goals and objectives, and that we are recognized and respected as part of that team.

Each person has these needs to different degrees. Each of these needs must be satisfied by the manager if the person is going to perform at his or her best. A deficiency or lack of satisfaction in any one of these needs, or the needs in Maslow's hierarchy, can cause your salespeople to perform at a lower level, often losing their enthusiasm for the work. Sometimes a lack of satisfaction even causes them to quit or leads to their needing to be fired or laid off.

Productive Sales Meetings

One of the most powerful tools you have for satisfying all of these needs simultaneously on an ongoing basis is the sales meeting. I have often turned sales organizations around by holding half-hour sales meetings at 8:00 a.m. every morning. During those thirty minutes, I call on each person to speak and to contribute. I tell the team about what the company is doing and what their goals are for the day, the week, and the month. I teach, train, and encourage. At the end of thirty minutes, people feel that their needs for dependence, independence, and interdependence have all been satisfied. They then go out and achieve wonderful sales results.

ACTION EXERCISES

1. What are the things that you could do or say to make your people feel happier, more secure, and more committed to the company?

2. Begin your next sales meeting by singling out specific individuals for praise and recognition for something they have accomplished.

THIRTEEN

Keep Them Focused

AS THE SALES manager, as the *officer-in-command* of your sales team, one of your key responsibilities is to keep your people focused on the most valuable activities they can engage in every day, all day long, to generate sales results.

According to a study done at Columbia University, the average salesperson only works about ninety minutes per day, approximately one and one-half hours. The rest of the day is spent warming up, cooling down, chatting with coworkers, playing on the Internet, drinking coffee, reading the newspaper, and going for coffee breaks and lunch.

We confirmed this statistic by providing a national sales team of 300 people with stopwatches to monitor the amount of time they actually worked. The company was astonished to find that, after a month of record keeping, the average salesperson was working ninety minutes and forty-two seconds per day.

When Are They Working?

When are your salespeople working? Only when they are ear-to-ear, face-to-face, with qualified prospects who can and will buy within a reasonable period of time. They are only working when they are prospecting, presenting, and closing. All the rest of the time, they are merely filling up space and engaging in non-revenue-generating activities.

A sales manager friend of mine worked for a major international corporation with 2,000 branches in more than 100 countries. After years as a salesperson and then sales supervisor, he was promoted to sales manager and given the task of turning around the worst-performing branch in the worldwide organization.

He traveled across the country to take his new position. On Monday morning, the first working day of the month, the thirty-two salespeople drifted into the office carrying their cups of Starbucks coffee and their newspapers. Every sales manager who had worked in this branch had been defeated and was forced to depart in disgrace. The salespeople assumed that this would be another sales manager that they would chew up and spit out.

A New Order of Business

They were wrong. That first day, the sales manager explained that there would be sales meetings at 8:00 a.m. each morning, then asked the question: "What do you notice that is not in this office?" No one had an answer. He said, "There are no customers in this office. If there are no customers in this office, you should not be in this office either. The sales meeting is now over. Please go out and call on customers."

On the second day, the salespeople discovered that all the desks and chairs in the office had been removed and sold overnight.

The new sales manager explained: "Since you will not be spending any time in this office during the day, you won't need any desks or chairs. We can have our morning sales meetings standing up. The sales meeting is now over. Good luck calling on customers and making sales. Have a good day!"

Within a month, twelve of the salespeople had quit. They refused to work under this "new regime." The others began to make more calls and more sales, upon which they received commissions. This energized them and created a higher level of motivation in the office that began to affect everyone.

Within six months, this branch had gone from number 2,000 (last place) to approximately number 1,000 in the world operation. Within two years, the branch had become the number one branch in the company in sales, paying the most commissions to its salespeople of any branch worldwide.

This is a true story. I told this story at a sales seminar a few years ago. At the break, one of the salespeople came up to me and confirmed it. He said, "I worked at that branch at that time, and I saw everything that happened. It was an unbeliev-able experience, and everything you said is perfectly true."

The 80/20 Rule

The 80/20 rule says that 20 percent of your activities will account for 80 percent of your results. Or said another way, it means that 80 percent of your activities will only account for 20 percent of your results. Nowhere is this truer than in sales and sales management.

In selling, 20 percent of your salespeople will account for 80 percent of your sales results. This means that the other 80 percent of your sales team only account for 20 percent of your sales results. You must discipline yourself to focus your time and attention on those top 20 percent of people on whom your business depends.

One of your responsibilities as a sales manager is to make sure that everyone is applying the 80/20 rule to every-thing they do.

Teach your salespeople that 80 percent of their business is going to come from 20 percent of the products and ser-vices that they offer. Eighty percent of their business is going to come from 20 percent of their prospects. Eighty percent of the profits that your company earns from sales results will come from 20 percent of the sales, and from 20 percent of your salespeople and customers.

The 20 percent of activities that account for 80 percent of sales results are *prospecting, presenting,* and *closing.* The most important job is to get ear-to-ear and face-to-face with qualified prospects. Your job is to make sure that your salespeople spend more and more time engaged in these specific activities.

When I started my sales career, someone shared with me a mantra that I used for several decades. It was this: Every minute of every day, ask yourself, as a salesperson, "Is what I am doing right now leading to a sale?"

If it is not leading to a sale, stop doing it immediately and begin right away to engage in activities that will lead to a sale. This mantra pushed me to the top of every sales force I ever joined, selling every product and service I represented over the years. This mantra has also helped countless thousands of salespeople become sales superstars. When everybody on your team practices this mantra, you are going to become a superstar sales manager.

ACTION EXERCISES

1. Teach your salespeople the 80/20 rule again and again, and help them become perfectly clear about the most important things they do all day long.

2. Buy stopwatches for each of your salespeople and have them keep track of how many minutes they spend face-to-face with customers each day for one month. Then set a goal to double the number of minutes the following month.

FOURTEEN

Use the CANEI Method

CANEI (continuous and never-ending improvement) as a philosophy is the driving force behind the most successful and profitable companies in the world today. It should be your philosophy as well.

With CANEI, you continually look for ways to improve every part of your performance, from the selection of salespeople through every aspect of managing and motivating them. You encourage your salespeople to improve as well, from the first customer contact to product delivery and customer satisfaction.

Quality circles are a popular use of the CANEI method. You bring your team together once each week to discuss improvements in sales methodology and effectiveness. The good news is that every single process in your business can be improved and should be improved continually. Sometimes one improvement in a key function can lead to a dramatic improvement in results. The most effective use of quality circles is to structure them around the key result areas in selling.

Seven Key Result Areas in Selling

There are seven key result areas in selling, plus one additional area:

1. Prospecting

2. Establishing rapport and trust

3. Identifying needs accurately

4. Presenting persuasively

5. Answering objections effectively

6. Closing the sale

7. Getting resales and referrals

The additional skill is time management for salespeople.

PROSPECTING

Give yourself a grade of one to ten on this key result area. How happy are you with the process of finding and developing new customers for your products and services? If you give yourself a low score here, this area can be the subject of a quality circle, where your team comes together to focus on methods and techniques to increase the quality and quantity of new prospects.

There is a principle in psychology that says that whatever you focus upon continually begins to improve, and sometimes quite rapidly. When you sit people down to discuss how they can improve in the area of new customer acquisition, they will come up with ideas that are working for them and that may be applicable to everyone in the sales force.

ESTABLISHING RAPPORT AND TRUST

You have heard it said that people don't care how much you know until they know how much you care. The ability of the salesperson to establish a high-quality relationship of trust and credibility is the absolutely essential starting point of the sales process.

Until customers are convinced that the salesperson cares about them more than making a sale, they will have little or no interest in meeting with or spending time with the salesperson. How could you improve your processes of building high trust and credibility quickly with new prospects?

IDENTIFYING NEEDS ACCURATELY

This is the process of asking preplanned questions, moving from the general to the specific, to uncover and identify the genuine wants and needs of a particular prospect. From the point of view of the customer, this is the most important part of the sales process in determining whether or not the customer will be interested and whether or not the customer will buy. How could you improve this questioning and discovery process?

PRESENTING PERSUASIVELY

According to thousands of customers who have been interviewed after making a purchase, the sale is actually made in the *presentation*. It is the way that the salesperson explains how the product or service can most benefit this particular customer, based on the previously identified wants and needs of the customer, that determines the sale more than any other factor. The good news is that all sales presentations can be improved in some way. How could your salespeople improve the quality of their presentations?

ANSWERING OBJECTIONS

There are no sales without objections. All customers have concerns about whether this product is the right one at the right price for them at this time. What are the most common objections that prospective customers use for holding back or refraining from buying? How could you answer or respond to these objections more effectively?

CLOSING THE SALE

Even the most promising prospect must be invited to buy. What are the low-pressure, no-pressure professional methods that are most effective in getting your interested prospects to take action and to actually buy and pay for your product or service? How could your closing methods be improved?

GETTING RESALES AND REFERRALS

The key to high profitability in any business is a steady stream of resales to happy, satisfied customers. In addition, referrals and recommendations from happy customers to new prospects and customers can be the most valuable and the most profitable part of the sales process. What is it that your salespeople do today to ensure high levels of after-sale customer satisfaction? How could you make your customers even happier in the future?

Time Management

The highest-paid and most productive salespeople manage their time more effectively than the lowest-paid and least productive ones do. What are the best time-planning and time-management techniques your highest-performing salespeople use every day? How can you teach, preach, and encourage your sales team to continually improve the quality of their time management so that they can improve the quantity of their sales results?

The Quality Circle Process

The best way to form quality circles is to establish a specific one-hour time period each week where the sales team gets together and focuses on a single part of the sales process and on a single question for continuous and never-ending improvement.

Have all of your salespeople explain how they have achieved the very best results in this specific key result area, and have them talk about how the "best practices" could be applied to their own sales activities.

The best time for a quality circle of this nature is either the first hour on Monday morning, so people can begin using the new ideas immediately, or the last hour on Friday afternoon at the end of a busy workweek, when people have just had a whole week of selling experiences.

Get Everyone Involved

Another way to use quality circles requires an interdisciplinary approach. You bring together people from all areas of your business, even the receptionist who answers customer phone calls, and have them all talk and share ideas on how you could improve both the sales process and the customer experience.

Bring in people from marketing, accounting, production, and shipping with their different viewpoints, and then talk about improvements and solutions. Be as specific and action-oriented as possible. Rather than saying to them, "Make customers happier," your directive to them should be something like, "Answer each customer call within two rings, and respond to customer inquiries within sixty minutes."

People develop high levels of loyalty and commitment to a company to the degree to which they feel they are involved in what the company is doing. The more that you involve your sales team members in the process of continuous improvement, the more dedicated, determined, and productive they will be.

ACTION EXERCISES

1. Make a decision today to carve out one hour each week for the team to come together and look for ways to improve performance in a specific sales activity.

2. Once you have agreed on a new idea for continuous and never-ending improvement, have everyone try it out immediately and report back with results. Do this every week on one key result area. You will be amazed at the cumulative results in improvements in sales performance.

FIFTEEN

Brainstorm for Sales Improvements

ONE OF YOUR key jobs as a sales manager is to release the full potential of each person that reports to you. As it happens, salespeople usually have an enormous reserve of potential that is seldom used and that can be released to increase sales results.

Brainstorming for sales improvements is a key job of the sales manager and one of the best ways to unleash the potential of your sales force. You should hold regular meetings with salespeople to brainstorm the solutions to specific problems facing the sales force, especially problems in dealing with difficult customers, changing competitive conditions, variations in demand for your products and services, and the daily difficulties that salespeople face that hold them back from achieving higher sales results.

Fortunately, as far back as 1945, some of the best thinkers in business have been working to perfect the process of brainstorming. They have come up with a series of rules and principles that you can use to get amazing results in short periods of time.

One of the most powerful ideas in business is the concept of "synergy." What this means is that a group of people working together in complete harmony can produce vastly more results than the sum total of the individuals if they were each working alone. This applies to brainstorming as well.

Idea Generation

You should consider holding brainstorming sessions on a regular basis, perhaps once per week, whenever there is a problem or an obstacle that is holding back sales generation and sales results.

The ideal time length for a brainstorming session is fifteen to forty-five minutes. When you organize such a session, you should start and stop on time, announcing exactly how long this session will be at the very beginning.

The brainstorming session should focus on a single question or problem that demands a practical answer, such as, "How can we increase our sales by 20 percent over the next ninety days?" Or, "How can we get more customers to buy faster than today?"

You can use brainstorming questions for each part of the sales process. For example, you could ask, "How can we find and set appointments with more qualified prospects than we are getting today?"

You can also ask, "What are three things that we could do in every initial meeting with a customer to build higher levels of rapport and trust?" The variety of questions you can ask is limited only by your imagination.

PROPER STRUCTURE

The best setup is a circular seating arrangement where everyone faces everyone else. When people can see, hear, and make eye contact with other people in a brainstorming session, they are more stimulated and motivated to contribute even more ideas.

The focus in each session is on the *quantity* of ideas rather than the quality of ideas. What experts in this field have found is that there is a direct relationship between the number of new ideas you generate and the likelihood that you will generate a great idea that can really make a difference in your business. Continually focus on generating as many ideas as possible by encouraging people to throw out every idea they can think of and put it on the table.

When I conduct brainstorming sessions for corporations, we always appoint two people in the session. The first is the *leader*. The job of the leader is to make sure that everyone around the table gets a chance to contribute their best ideas. People who may be a little bit more self-contained or shy about speaking up in front of others must especially be encouraged to give their best ideas. Often, the person who says very little is the one who comes up with the groundbreaking idea that changes the entire sales results of the business.

The second person is the *recorder*. This is the person whose primary job is to write down every idea as it is suggested, as quickly as possible. In some brainstorming sessions where there may be six or seven people at the table, you may require two or even three people to act as recorders to keep up with the many new ideas being generated.

FEWER PEOPLE, BETTER RESULTS

The ideal number of people for a brainstorming session is five to seven. Less than five people diminishes the potential value of the brainstorming session, as well as the number of ideas. When you have more than seven people, not everyone gets a chance to make a full contribution to the session.

The key to successful brainstorming is to suspend judgment completely. No comments or criticisms are allowed, no matter how strange or crazy an idea might sound initially. Very often, combining one ridiculous idea with another ridiculous idea yields an absolutely brilliant idea that can really make a difference to results.

You should stop the brainstorming session at exactly the time that you had originally announced. The pressure of a deadline increases the number of good ideas.

Idea Evaluation

The brainstorming session is divided into two parts. Part one is idea generation (as described previously), and part two is idea evaluation.

Once you have generated a sufficient number of ideas and written down each of them, you can then evaluate them one by one. When I have conducted brainstorming sessions on a single question, with several tables of five to seven people, we will often collect the ideas from one table and pass them on to the next table for the evaluation part of the process. This way, no one evaluating the ideas from the other table has any ego investment in being right or wrong or having the ideas accepted or rejected.

In evaluating ideas, you go through them, discuss them, and select those ideas that seem to have the greatest possibilities for immediate application and improved results. There is a direct relationship between the amount of participation and discussion, on the one hand, and the amount of involvement and commitment to the company, on the other. The more people get a chance to contribute their very best thinking to improving the results of their jobs, the more loyal and motivated they will be, doing their jobs even better in the future.

Unlock Their Creative Potential

Brainstorming is one of the most powerful ways to motivate your staff members, to get them thinking creatively, and to keep them continually involved in helping you come up with even more solutions to do the job better.

Everyone has ideas. Over the years, I have taught brainstorming in organizations across the country. I have been astonished at the quality and quantity of the ideas that come from executive assistants, clerks, junior employees, and others who may have limited experience in the business or exposure to the market. Some of their ideas were worth many thousands and even tens of thousands of dollars.

Perhaps the greatest benefit of regular brainstorming sessions is the effect that they will have on you personally. You will be brighter, sharper, and more creative, most of the time. You will be perceived to be a better, more competent, and more capable manager than you would be if you were not conducting regular brainstorming sessions. You will be building a peak performance sales team on a daily and a weekly basis by asking your salespeople to contribute their very best ideas to help achieve the sales goals of the company.

ACTION EXERCISES

1. Select one problem, question, or goal that seems to be a concern of everyone on your team.

2. Decide immediately to arrange your first brainstorming session, perhaps even later today. As Michael Jordan and Nike have famously said, "Just do it!"

SIXTEEN

Discipline Salespeople Effectively

ONE OF YOUR primary goals as the sales manager is to create a peak performance sales team. This is only possible when your salespeople perform at the highest levels possible, which requires discipline.

The best athletes, and the best players on your team, are the ones who most enjoy and appreciate the rigors of highly disciplined work and conduct.

When you set high standards and discipline your sales staff to meet those standards on a regular basis, you are doing each person on the team an incredible favor. Many people look back in their lives to a tough boss who was demanding in terms of performance. This person changed their whole attitude toward themselves and their work. As a result, they were more successful working under that boss, and later in other jobs and endeavors, than they ever would have been without that discipline.

Discipline Defined

My favorite definition of self-discipline comes from Elbert Hubbard: "Self-discipline is the ability to make yourself do what you should do, whether you feel like it or not."

It doesn't take any discipline to do something if you already feel like doing it, but it takes a lot of discipline when you would much rather be doing something else. It takes discipline to do things that require hard work, persistence, and determination. Self-discipline is the only way to build character and personal excellence. Discipline is the key to building a peak performance team of any kind, especially a sales team.

Jim Rohn said, "Success is tons of discipline." He also said, "Discipline weighs ounces; regret weighs tons."

Zig Ziglar said, "If you will be hard on yourself, life will be easy on you. But if you insist on being easy on yourself, life is going to be very hard on you."

Set Clear Standards of Performance

The correct approach to disciplining people begins long before a need for a disciplinary conversation arises. It begins with your setting clear standards of performance and goals that everyone knows, understands, and agrees to.

When you set clear goals and standards, you must make it clear that these are definite standards with specific timelines.

They are not voluntary or arbitrary. They are not a matter of choice or discretion on the part of the salesperson. You must make it plain from the beginning that people who cannot or do not meet these standards and deadlines will have to move on and make way for other people who are willing to rise to the standards of performance required.

To maintain discipline in your organization, you must review performance regularly, at least weekly and often daily. As discussed in Chapter 11 on planning sales activities, you should have clear action plans for each person on your team. These plans should include the number of new customer calls salespeople are expected to make each day and each week, the number of customers they are expected to meet with or speak to, the number of presentations they are expected to give, and ultimately, the size and number of sales that are required to keep this job.

Conduct Performance Appraisals

When I started off as a sales manager, having worked under some very difficult bosses, I was of the opinion that the purpose of the performance appraisal was to criticize the salesperson for poor performance and demand that the person do better. The turning point in my management life came when I realized that the real purpose of performance appraisal is not to punish, but to improve performance.

How do you improve performance? The only way that you can do it is by helping people feel more confident and competent about themselves *after* the meeting than they were *before*. Whenever you criticize or condemn poor behavior, you actually increase the likelihood of it occurring again. You make people so nervous and afraid of subsequent criticism that they actually decrease their sales efforts and activities, not increase them.

The rule is always to praise in public and appraise in private. There should only be the two of you present when you give negative performance feedback to another person. This saves the person from embarrassment and makes it far more likely that the individual will take action to improve after the meeting.

Explain Your Concerns

Begin by explaining that you have a concern about the person's performance. Use "I" messages rather than "you" messages. Say things like, "I am concerned that your sales numbers are not where I expected them to be at this point."

By using these words, you put the focus on the sales numbers rather than on the salesperson. You discuss the sales numbers as if they belong to someone else. You evaluate the sales numbers objectively and unemotionally, mutually seeking a way to get them to improve. This reduces the fear and stress of a performance appraisal and allows the salesperson to discuss ways of improving the numbers without becoming emotional.

The most powerful words you can use in performance appraisal are the words *next time* and *in the future*. For example, when you are talking about the sales performance not being as high as you expected it to be, you can ask whether "in the future" the person might do this or that. Or you can say, "Next time this happens, why don't you try this [and give an example of a particular strategy]?"

Whenever you point attention to the future, which is a period of time that people can do something about, you give them hope and optimism. When you criticize people for past performance, they often feel trapped and become angry and defensive.

Be Clear About the Problem

Agree on the problem that exists, whether it is poor time management, lack of prospecting activity, or failure to close the sale, and agree on a plan to improve performance in that area. Ask specifically what the person is going to do more of, or less of. What is the salesperson going to start doing, or stop doing? Make notes during the conversation so that you have a written record of what was agreed upon.

Offer to help the salesperson with additional training, support, and coaching. Very often a salesperson is lacking a particular skill that is sabotaging the entire sales process. Very often a single audio program, video training program, or a live seminar can transform a salesperson from a mediocre performer to a sales leader.

Think About Solutions

Keep thinking about what you can do to help your salespeople perform better. Remember that one of your key jobs as a sales manager is to train, coach, counsel, and be a helper.

Be firm but fair. Don't allow people off the hook. Once they have agreed to what they are going to do more of or less of, make sure that they do it. Check in with them on a regular basis, daily if necessary. Be a kind person, but a strict disciplinarian. This, above all, is what your salespeople need from you.

Always insist on high standards of conduct and performance.

ACTION EXERCISES

1. Identify one of your problem salespeople and arrange to sit down privately and discuss sales performance and what you could do to help the salesperson improve.

2. Make sure that all of your salespeople have clear, specific performance standards for each day and each week, written down, and that they submit regular sales reports to you.

SEVENTEEN

Let Your Poor Performers Go

DESCRIBING ONE of the seven keys to building a great company, Jim Collins, in his book *Good to Great*, said: "Get the right people on the bus. Get the wrong people off the bus. And then get the right people into the right seats on the bus."

The most stressful part of a sales manager's life is letting people go and firing poor performers. The second most stressful part of a manager's life is being fired yourself.

We say, "If you don't get some experience with the first, you are going to get some experience with the second." If you cannot let go of poor performers, you will eventually be replaced by someone who can. Peter Drucker wrote, "A manager who keeps an incompetent person in place is himself incompetent and does not deserve the position of manager."

The fact is that in the world of selling, about one-third of new people will work out and become reasonably successful, if not sales stars. About one-third will be average performers. And one-third will not work out at all, either immediately or over the long term. This is why there is a churn of about 30 percent of salespeople each year. It is like change—inevitable, unavoidable, and never-ending.

The Dehiring Process

The rule in business is that "everybody knows everything." This means that everybody in your office knows the relative level of competence and ability of everyone else. One of the fastest ways to demotivate a sales team is to keep a poor performer in place. This tells everyone that poor performance is rewarded with a regular paycheck and excellent performance is given an occasional pat on the head.

When an employee cannot do the job, for whatever reason, you will have to be ready to deal with it. You must be ready to step up and do what is necessary to ensure a peak-performing sales team for your company.

Once you have decided to let someone go, make a firm decision about exactly when and where you are going to do it. The best time to fire people is early in the week. This gives them an opportunity to go out and start looking for a new job immediately. If you fire people on a Friday, there is nothing they can do but go home and become depressed and angry. This is neither kind nor necessary.

Once you have decided to fire a person, never fire in *anger*. You are not angry with the person. There is no negativity involved. The job has not worked out. It is unfortunate, but it is an inevitable fact of life. Always be calm, cool, and gentle in the firing process.

Protect the self-esteem of the person being let go in every way possible. This means that you never criticize, condemn, or bring up the past. It is too late for that. The term of employment is over. Whatever the person has done or not done in the past is irrelevant. Do not bring it into the discussion. Do not get into an argument over "he said, she said."

Jack Welch was clear about always firing people in a low-key, gentle, and professional way. He taught that you will never know how the world turns. It may be that you will be applying for a job to work under this person at some time in the future. Don't leave any enemies behind you.

Broken Record

The simplest way to fire is to use the broken record method. This method requires that you simply repeat a statement over and over again, like a broken record, until the other person finally accepts the statement. I have taught this process to more than a million managers worldwide, and thousands of them have reported back to me how powerful and effective it really is.

You sit down with the person you are going to fire and say these words: "Bill, I have given this a lot of thought. I have come to the conclusion that this is not the right job for you, and you are not the right person for this job. And I think you would be happier doing something else."

Notice the wording. When you say "I have given this a lot of thought," you are making it clear that this is not a knee-jerk decision that you are making out of anger or frustration.

Second, you say, "I have come to the conclusion that this is not the right job for you, and that you are not the right person for this job." These two statements are completely true. The salesperson already knows that this is not the right job for him; it is clear because the person has been unable to do the job in a satisfactory way.

BE CALM BUT DETERMINED

Some managers have told me that sometimes they had to repeat these words ten and twenty times before the salesperson (who was never this tenacious before) finally accepted that the decision had been made and was irrevocable. At that point, the salesperson often thanks the manager for his time and patience, and accepts that the job is over and that it's time to move on.

It is at this stage, when people accept that their job has been terminated, that you then offer them whatever severance plan you have decided upon in advance. The basic rule is one week of pay for every year of employment. You can be more or less generous, depending on your company policies and how you feel about this particular individual.

Once people have agreed to leave and accepted that their job is terminated, help them save face. Create a cover story in which you agree that they will be allowed to "resign for personal reasons."

From that day onward, you must discipline yourself to keep your mouth shut. If anyone ever asks you why this person left the company, you should look the questioner straight in the eye and say, "Bill decided to leave for personal reasons." Never say anything negative or derogatory about a person you have fired. This can come back to haunt you, especially in a court of law.

TAKE THE FINAL ACTION

When you fire people, you usually have them leave the premises at once. Have someone supervise them to clear out their desk and belongings and transfer over all credit cards, keys, and computer codes. Do not leave them alone for a minute after you have fired them. No phone calls. No conversations. Take them to the door and show them out, and wish them well.

If the separation is not amicable, or you feel any reason to distrust this person, change the locks that very day, and change all access codes for your computer network and the Internet immediately.

Your Personal Responsibility

Just as hiring is 95 percent of your success in building an effective sales team, firing people is also an essential part of your job as a sales manager. It goes with the job description. It is seldom easy to let people go, and it can often be painful and emotional. But this is something that you owe your company, your other salespeople, and especially yourself.

ACTION EXERCISES

1. Ask the zero-based thinking question: Is there anyone working for you today who, knowing what you now know, you would not hire back again today, if you had to do it over?

2. The rule is that the best time to fire a person is the first time that it crosses your mind. If there is anyone on your sales team who you would not hire again today, decide immediately to let the person go by following the process described in this chapter. You will be both relieved and happy at the result.

EIGHTEEN

Lead by Example

PERHAPS THE most important activity you engage in, every hour of every day, is to be a role model. As a role model, you have to set an example for your staff. You have to set high standards for yourself and then maintain those standards.

Before you became a sales manager, you were part of the sales team. You spoke to, interacted with, socialized with, and spent time with other salespeople. You saw yourself and thought about yourself as a salesperson. You identified with other salespeople and related to them on a personal basis.

But when you become a manager, you become a part of *management*. Your primary loyalties are not to your coworkers and colleagues anymore, but to your managers and your boss—the people who have entrusted you with this position.

Your World Has Changed

As a manager, virtually overnight, everything has changed. Everyone is watching you. Everyone is observing everything that you do or say. Every look, glance, frown, or opinion that you express is quickly relayed to everyone on the sales team. Your actions and behaviors, from the minute you walk in the door to the minute you leave, can raise the motivation and loyalty of your sales force or diminish it. Nothing that you do or say is neutral anymore. You are now the person in charge of their paychecks and their futures, and everyone is watching.

The rule is that your salespeople only become better when you become better.

If you want your salespeople to be better disciplined, more organized, and punctual, you must raise the bar on yourself. You must become better disciplined, more organized, and more punctual.

The Timeless Questions

Perhaps the most powerful questions I have ever heard in terms of developing yourself to be a better role model are the following:

1. What kind of a country would my country be if everyone in it was just like me?

If this question were asked and answered in the context of political debate and policy discussions, the outcomes and results would be very different from many of the national and statewide political decisions being made today.

2. What kind of a family would my family be if everyone in it was just like me?

Answering this question and taking action on your answer can have a major impact on your family in many different respects.

3. What kind of a company would my company be if everyone in it was just like me?

When you ask this question, if you are honest, you will see that there is always room for improvement. Sometimes just changing one key behavior can make a big difference in the performance of your sales team.

Identify One Characteristic

One of my friends is considered to be the top management coach in the United States. He works only with the key executives in Fortune 1,000 companies. He is brought in by the CEO or the board of directors to work with a problem executive who, aside from one or two personality faults, is a highly skilled performer.

He explained to me that when he works with executives, he helps them identify one or two personality characteristics that are interfering with their ability to maximize the productivity of the people that report to them. He uses a proven process to help executives learn or unlearn one or two qualities over the course of twelve months. What he found was that, if these qualities (or lack thereof) are interfering with the executive's effectiveness, then either developing or unlearning them would have a dramatic impact on the quality and quantity of results that the executive was getting in his position.

This lesson can also apply to you. It is almost impossible for you to change your basic personality, but you can develop or unlearn a single quality that might be just enough to dramatically improve your effectiveness and productivity.

If you are not sure of the answers to any of the timeless questions that might allow you to develop into a better role model, then you need to have the courage to ask for input from the people with whom you interact every day.

Ask for Input and Feedback

Ask your key staff if there is anything that you should start doing or stop doing that would allow you to be more effective as a manager. Ask your spouse or children if there is anything that they would like you to do more of or less of to be a better family member. You will often be amazed at the answers that you get. And what you do with these answers can have a major impact on your future.

Coming back to your sales team, how would it be if they all worked like you and managed their time the way you do? How would they perform if they planned their days the way you do and interacted with others the same way that you do? What would they be like if their habits of learning and personal development, punctuality and attentiveness, followup and follow-through, were identical to yours?

Select One Behavior to Change

If you are honest, you will probably notice a lot of areas where you can improve. But don't try to do everything at once. Instead, select one new habit or behavior that you could work on that would allow you to be more effective in the weeks ahead.

For example, one of the most negative behaviors of executives, according to the research, is that they interrupted continually when other people were speaking. When they held meetings, they would throw out their own ideas when someone else was in the middle of a sentence or expressing an idea. As a result, fewer and fewer people said anything at the meetings. The executives would talk the entire time, ask if there were any further questions, and close the meeting. Then they would wonder why no one spoke up in the office and they were kept unaware of what was really going on.

Just developing the habits of asking good questions, listening attentively, and making tentative suggestions can dramatically improve your effectiveness and the entire performance of your sales team.

Resolve to develop one new habit at a time, even if it takes you several months to lock that new habit in and make it a fixed part of your personality. As Shakespeare said, "Make haste slowly." If you simply develop one or two good managerial behaviors each year—behaviors that make you a more effective and a better role model to your staff—the cumulative effect over the months and years ahead could transform your career.

Remember, once you become a manager, nothing is neutral. Everything you do or say, or fail to do or say, has an impact on the members of your sales team. One of the marks of superior managers is that they are always aware of the impact of their words and behaviors on other people.

ACTION EXERCISES

1. Ask one of the people at work, someone you like and trust, "Is there anything I could do more of or less of that would make me a better sales manager?"

2. Select one behavior that you would like to change, or one habit that you would like to develop, and begin work on that until you are successful.

NINETEEN

The Control Valve on Performance

ONE OF THE most important jobs you do for your company is to attract, keep, and build a high-performance sales force. According to the most detailed research, the job of the sales manager is the "pivotal skill" in the sales-driven organization like yours. The better you do your job in building a sales team, the healthier and more profitable is the entire company.

When salespeople were interviewed and asked, "What was the primary reason that you took that job?" they almost all gave the same answer: "Because of the sales manager."

An additional reason that people give for taking a sales job is because they will get excellent training, which will help them make more sales and earn more money. But this begins with how confident they feel about the sales manager in the first place.

The Reason for Staying

Salespeople were asked a second question: "Why have you stayed with a particular company when there may have been other, better opportunities for you in the industry or in the market?"

The answer was almost always, "I stayed at the job because of my sales manager. I liked him, trusted him, and felt comfortable in that company." The research shows that it is quite common for some salespeople to join a company and stay there for decades because of the high-quality relationship with the sales manager.

When top performers left a sales organization and went to the competition, they were asked a third question: "Why did you leave that job?" The answer was almost always, "Because the sales manager was difficult to deal with, critical, and untrustworthy."

You Are the Control Valve

The relationship between the salesperson and the sales manager is the control valve on performance. Nothing is more important than what is called "the moment of truth" when the salesperson and the sales manager interact, either face-to-face, in meetings, on the telephone, or even by email.

It is that point of communication and the emotional nature of that point of contact that largely determines the performance of the salesperson in the marketplace.

If the relationship between salespeople and their sales manager is positive, happy, and supportive, the salespeople will usually perform at the very best level that they are capable of. If the relationship is negative or critical, the level of performance of the salesperson can drop immediately, sometimes for several days, and sometimes for as long as that person works for that company.

How can you tell if you have created a positive, successful, and high-performance sales environment? Simple. The very fact that you like your salespeople causes them to like themselves even more and to be more persistent and determined to achieve excellent sales results.

Create a Great Place to Work

Each year, the Great Place to Work Institute, in conjunction with *Fortune* magazine, produces a report called "The 100 Best Companies to Work For." (You can check their website: www.greatplacetowork.com.) Each year they survey thousands of employees of hundreds of companies to find out who are the happiest and most productive.

When employees of top companies are asked, "What makes your company a great place to work?" they give very similar answers across all industries. For a company to be a great place to work, the number one ingredient mentioned is "high trust."

When asked what they mean by "high trust," employees say that in their company, they feel they can say whatever they want to say, and make mistakes in their work, without fear of being reprimanded or criticized or losing their jobs. As a result, they feel comfortable and happy. They are more relaxed and creative, and they perform at much higher levels.

One of your goals as a sales manager is to create a great place to work. The positive work environment can have more of an effect on sales results than almost any other factor.

One of my clients was a company with eighteen branches. One of the branches had the highest sales volume, both individually and overall of any branch in the organization. And everyone knew the reason why. It was because the sales manager was a remarkable man. People applied to and crawled over each other to get transferred into that office because they knew that under that sales manager, their sales would double and triple within a few months.

The best sales managers that I have known over the years have a steady stream of high-performing salespeople coming to them looking to change jobs. They interview and apply well in advance. The sales manager has a list, a file of potential sales candidates who are just biding time and waiting for an opportunity to move over.

ACTION EXERCISES

1. What specific actions can you take to make your salespeople glad that they are working for you rather than someone else?

2. How exactly would you like to be described by people in your business and in your market? What words would you like people to use in describing you? What could you start doing immediately to ensure that people use those words?

TWENTY

Four Keys to Building Salespeople

THERE ARE four practices that you can engage in daily that will motivate your salespeople to higher levels of performance.

1. Unconditional Positive Regard

This is perhaps the greatest gift that one person can give to another. This is true between spouses, between parents and children, between friends and family, and in all other relationships.

Almost everyone grows up with fears of failure, rejection, and self-doubt. As the result of destructive criticism in early childhood, the greatest single emotional affliction is the feeling that "I'm not good enough." This feeling affects every part of life and reduces performance, effectiveness, happiness, and productivity.

However, when people feel that they are completely liked and accepted, without judgment, evaluation, or criticism by other people, they feel relaxed, comfortable, and happy about themselves.

Remember, people's level of self-esteem determines their level of performance as well. Everything that you do to express unconditional positive regard and acceptance of another person causes that person's self-esteem to increase and self-image to improve. As a result, the other person becomes more positive and persistent in everything she does, including and especially in sales-related activities.

The reverse of unconditional positive regard is to criticize, complain, or condemn someone for something that he either did or did not do. One negative word or glance from you can reduce a person's productivity for the whole day. Always be positive and supportive.

2. Physical Contact

People are greatly affected by physical contact with others. It can be as simple as a warm handshake when you see a person each day. It can be a pat on the shoulder when a person has done or said something good, or even as you pass by each other in the hallway. Lightly touching a person's arm or hand in the course of a conversation makes the other person feel more valuable and closer to you.

In sales psychology, I have found that if you just touch the customer's hand when making a point or when you are sharing a laugh together, the customer will like and trust you far more. In controlled studies, when salespeople were instructed to touch a customer below the elbow and the customer was asked about it later, most customers did not recall that touching ever happened. They just liked the salesperson more and were more open to the salesperson's offer.

This is true in all human relationships. A handshake, a pat on the shoulder or back, a touch on the hand or wrist, all convey a message of warmth, trust, and confidence in the other person.

3. Eye Contact

Stephen Covey, in his book *The Seven Habits of Highly Effective People*, pointed out that each person has an emotional tank that needs to be filled on a regular basis with positive messages and positive contact from other people. He said that each time you make a deposit in the emotional tank, the person feels happier, more positive, and more valuable.

He also pointed out that each time you criticize people or say something negative to them, it drains their emotional tank and creates an emotional deficit that you will have to make up if they are going to return to high levels of performance.

One of the ways that you can fill the emotional tank of another person is through eye contact. Listen to your salespeople intently when they want to talk. Resist the urge to comment or to add your own observations. Face them directly, look into their eyes, nod, smile, and make it clear that you very much value them and what they are saying.

You always pay attention to those people and things that you most value. When you pay close attention to another person by giving them warm, genuine eye contact when they speak, they feel more valuable and important and tend to be the very best people they can possibly be.

4. Focused Attention

Focused attention makes the salesperson feel valued and important. You show focused attention when you practice the four key listening skills.

First, *listen attentively* without interrupting. Face the person directly, lean forward, and pay attention as if there was nothing else in the world you would rather do right now than hear what this person has to say.

Second, *pause* before replying. When the other person pauses, either to reorganize thoughts or to hear what you have to say, pause and leave a silence of three to five seconds, or even longer. When you pause, you gain three advantages. First, you avoid the risk of interrupting the other person, who may just be preparing to continue. Second, you show the person that what he has said is important and you are giving it careful consideration. Third, you actually understand what the person is saying, thinking, and feeling at a deeper level of mind. And you get all of this from pausing.

Third, *question* for clarification. Never assume that you completely understand what the other person really said or meant by what she said. Instead, ask the question, "How do you mean?" Then wait patiently for the answer. The other person will expand on what she just said, giving you more opportunity to listen and to build self-esteem in the other person.

Remember that the person who asks questions has control. The more questions you ask in a conversation, and the more attentively you listen, the more you actually control the flow of the conversation and the emotions of the other person. Asking questions is a powerful conversational technique that gives you an opportunity to listen more and sell more.

Fourth, *feed it back* in your own words. This is called "the acid test" of listening. This is where you demonstrate that you were actually listening when the other person was speaking, rather than thinking of something else and waiting for the person to stop talking.

Say something like, "So let me make sure that I understand what you're saying. What you are saying is this, and what you really mean is that. Is that correct?"

When you can feed back to people exactly what they have said to you, in your own words, you prove to them that you were really listening closely. You prove to them that you were really paying attention because you really value them and what they have to say.

The self-concept and self-image of your salespeople is determined by the way you treat them each day. So treat your people well. Everything that you do or say raises or lowers their self-esteem and, ultimately, their sales performance. Make sure that everything you do in every interaction with your salespeople leaves your employees feeling better off about themselves than before they spoke to you.

ACTION EXERCISES

1. Select one of your salespeople and practice "focused attention" on him or her. Ask a couple of questions about how the person is doing, how she is feeling, and what she thinks about the current market. Then listen attentively and intently to the person's answers.

2. Each time you make contact with a person, each day, shake hands, look the person straight in the eye and smile, or touch his hand or arm lightly to show that you are happy to see him. You may be astonished at the results.

TWENTY-ONE

Courage, the Vital Quality of Success

COURAGE IS THE single most important quality of leadership. And courage comes from acting courageously whenever courage is required.

Sales management is a tough job, and it requires a special kind of person to succeed at it. Your decision to stay the course, to "keep on keeping on" no matter how tough it gets, is the true mark of courage and character. Persistence is the one quality that will inevitably guarantee your success. And persistence is the demonstration of courage.

Self-Control Is Necessary

It is lonely at the top as a sales manager. But you do not have the luxury of sharing your problems, concerns, and fears with your salespeople. You must keep these things away from your staff. Keep your misgivings about the business climate or about other people to yourself. Sharing them with your sales staff will only demoralize them.

You've heard the song lyric that says, "Smile even though your heart is breaking." No matter how you feel on the inside, you must discipline yourself to be cheerful and confident on the outside. This is a key requirement of leadership.

Your position as a sales manager can be richly rewarding. It can be the springboard to high achievement in life and in business. Many of the top executives of the biggest companies came up through sales management. They earned their spurs on the battlefield of competitive sales activity.

You need courage every day to face the inevitable ups and downs of your profession.

Pray for Peace, Hope for War

Remember this: When the situation is the worst of all, there are great opportunities for you to learn and grow. There is an old saying in the military: "Soldiers pray for peace, but hope for war."

This is because nobody wants war and all of the pain and suffering involved. They pray for peace, as all reasonable people do. But soldiers hope for war as well because it is only during warfare that rapid promotion through the ranks is possible.

Applied to your job as a sales manager, the more problems you are struggling with, the bigger your difficulties, the tougher the competition, and the greater your challenges, the more likely it is that you are on the fast track to rapid growth, development, and success.

Remember that you cannot advance quickly if everything is going smoothly. You can only advance and move up when you are contending against a sea of troubles and overcoming them.

Remember these beautiful lines by the late Dean LeBaron Russell Briggs of Harvard:

> Do your work. Not just your work and no more, but that little bit more for the lavishing's sake—that little bit more that is worth all the rest. And if you suffer, as you will, and if you doubt, as you must, do your work. Put your heart into it, and the sky will clear. Then out of your very suffering and doubt will be born the supreme joy of life.

You have within yourself the ability to become one of the great sales managers of your generation. When you practice these tools, techniques, and ideas, you will get better and better. Your sales force will become better, stronger, and more capable of getting sales results. You will achieve all of your goals in your business life.